▼

Pinches of Salt

SPIRITUAL SEASONINGS

Peggy L. "Shriver "

▲

Foreword by
William Sloane Coffin

Acknowledgment is made for permission to print the following poems:

"Anno Domini," copyright 1980, The Christian Century Foundation, and reprinted by permission from the January 24, 1979, issue of *The Christian Century;* and "The Spirit of 34th Street," copyright 1980, The Christian Century Foundation, and reprinted by permission from the December 24, 1980, issue of *The Christian Century.*

The text of "A Prayer for Life's Seasons, Young People's Choir, Youth Choir, SATB, Choir and Keyboard" (herein "A Prayer for Life's Seasons"), copyright 1988 by Galaxy Music Corp., Boston. Music by Alex Wyton and text by Peggy L. Shriver. Reprinted by permission.

"Fill Us with Vision," copyright © 1989 by Hope Publishing Company, Carol Stream, IL 60188. All Rights Reserved. Used by Permission.

"A Politic Proposal." Reprinted with permission from *The Bible Vote: Religion and the New Right,* by Peggy L. Shriver. The Pilgrim Press, copyright 1981, New York, NY.

"Airplane Landing" and "Eucharist," first printed in *The Reformed Journal,* vol. 39, issue 3 (March, 1989); and "Tales of India," first printed in *The Reformed Journal,* vol. 39, issue 5 (May, 1989). Reprinted by permission.

Book design by Jim Gerhard

First edition

Published by Westminster/John Knox Press
Louisville, Kentucky

PRINTED IN THE UNITED STATES OF AMERICA
9 8 7 6 5 4 3 2 1

Library of Congress Cataloging-in-Publication Data

Shriver, Peggy L.
  Pinches of salt : spiritual seasonings / Peggy L. Shriver.
— 1st ed.
      p.   cm.
  ISBN 0-664-25159-5

  1. Christian poetry, American.   I. Title.
PS3569.H743P5   1990
811'.54—dc20   90-35143
                                                      CIP

▼

Pinches of Salt

▲

CONTENTS

III. DIALOGUE

IV. ABYSSES AND ALIENATIONS

V. MOMENTS OF GRACE

VI. FINITUDE

VII. HOPE

In gratitude
I dedicate this harvest of poems
to all those who,
by entering my life,
brought poetry into it,
most especially

    my parents,
        my husband,
            my children.

    Peggy Ann Leu Shriver
    1990

Foreword

Believe it or not, there are people who do not read a poem a day. If, dear reader, you are among them, the book you hold in your hands will help you mend your ways.

Good poetry, like goodness itself, is unpretentious. Peggy Shriver's poems, while vivid, are exceptionally free of pretense. But they are deceptively simple and must be read more than once to feel the full impact of their gentle subversion. For without raising (or ostentatiously lowering) her voice, Shriver summons us to be ill-fitted to the conventions and categories of our culture. She regularly compares a fundamental vision of life with God to today's attractive, secular view of reality that flatters our prejudices and betrays our interests. She shares the insight of the Russian theologian Nicolas Berdyaev, who wrote, "Once bread is assured, God becomes a hard and inescapable reality, instead of an escape from harsh reality."

In Shriver's poems that are less explicitly religious, there is still tension of the kind that reflects English poet William Blake's understanding that

> Joy and woe are woven fine
> A clothing for the soul divine.

And Shriver's piety accords with Blake's conclusion:

> And when this we rightly know
> Safely through the world we go.

Christians are often brought up short by the realization that the most memorable passages in scripture are in the indicative, not the imperative. Likewise, good poetry describes far more than it exhorts. Shriver may lead us, but always with a light rein, giving us our head. Or, we might say, she is a good shepherd of the Eastern persuasion, the kind who lead their sheep rather than drive them as do Western shepherds. In any case, hungry sheep will here find food. As one of them, I am deeply grateful to Peggy Shriver.

March 5, 1990   William Sloane Coffin

Introduction

Turning this sheaf of poems into a book has been like gathering a field of wild flowers into a florist's formal flower arrangement. They were written in scattered, precious moments of my life with no thought of how they might nestle against one another in the pages of a book. But the gathering and the arranging have been instructive even to the author.

Although written over a stretch of more than thirty-five years, certain themes have found varied expression often enough to merit grouping under such obviously theological titles as "grace" and "hope" or "alienation." Most of the "incarnation" poems were written as one more annual effort to speak a word of Christmas to friends—a bit daunting, but surprisingly fertile with new possibility each year. Other poems arose from unique moments in my life that often shared a remarkable human universality—birth, death, illness, old age, parenthood, leaving home, and marriage. Love in marriage is so joyously profound that it is offered very sparingly in this collection.

While some poems connect me with the great sweeping drama of human life and call out images and language of faith, others are little dramas within themselves (like "Spirit of 34th Street," a true happening) that fit into a larger context of religious meaning. Frequently I did not set out to write "religious verse," as is evident in some of the poems in this collection. But sometimes the religious lens through which I view the world took over, while some poems were an explicit attempt to think theologically—Easter and Christmas poems especially.

A number of poems speak to social issues like war, poverty, racism, and brokenness, but they are fragments that cannot and ought not preach a complete line of argument. Others respond to the natural world in its otherness and awe, a world both beautiful and terrifying. Travels to distant places introduce some strange names and images, pose some fresh issues of Christian faith or connect with some familiar ones ("Dar es Salaam," "Kinshasha Ivory Market," "The Bull Leapers of Knossos"). Only recently have I sought to try the discipline of hymnody in collaboration with a musician ("A Prayer for Life's Seasons," for example).

Few poems speak directly of or to Jesus Christ, yet without him the poems would be decidedly different. Jesus is always pointing me toward the God "clothed in majesty," while reminding me that God knows me by my name as I am invited to know God's. Thus the ordinary things of life can be filled with exultation. Life in the presence of God is seasoned with "Pinches of Salt" that preserve, enhance and bring savor to daily existence.

Poems often nag themselves into existence. Something troubles, doesn't "feel right," bears down or lifts up, until the words are shaped into a discovered meaning (as in "Auction Trespassers"). Months may pass before something I want to say takes form, even something as deeply disturbing as viewing my mother in her casket. For some events of deep emotion or spirituality, I am still waiting for the right words, shape, images. Some will remain with the Spirit as "sighs too deep for words."

March 1990   P. L. S.
New York City

▼

I

Incarnation

▲

Mary's Christmas

He was so small,
this child I feared for,
    marveled at
    and loved
from the moment that his presence
    was announced
    to me.
I wrapped him from the cold,
    the roughness of the straw,
    the strange vigil
    of beasts.

Joseph and I,
we had no plans to notify
    our neighbors of
    his birth.
Yet somehow people knew.
Timid shepherds left their flocks
    to gaze
    at us.
Rich strangers journeyed far
    to see
    our child.
He was our child,
    yet claimed
    by all.

Portraits were a luxury
    beyond
    our means.
I did not need an artist
    to engrave
    his image in
    my heart.
You, too, are welcome
    to behold
    my son.
Fashion him as your
    imagining
    requires.

Transforming him, you are yourself
   transformed,
freed to find his face in
   everyone.

▼

Cornucopia and Christ

The span between Thanksgiving
and the birth of Christ
is measured out in shopping days,
rounded at each end by turkey feasts.
More pertinent than candles,
televised balloon parades of bloated fantasies
symbolize the Advent of the holidays,
Thanksgiving cornucopias
and Santa's bulging bag seeming
less the magnanimity of God
than human generosity.

Yet, for the faithful,
gratitude and joy connect these holidays,
as thankfulness for harvest past
begins the exultation
for the greatest gift of all.
Creation and Creator dance
in field and orchard, marketplace and farm,
a prelude to the manger mystery
of God-with-us.

Christmas Courage

A Berkshire night inescapably displays
    a clear Copernican sky.
Crickets and tree frogs pulse
    with our pounding hearts
as we contemplate
    the blinking labyrinth of space.

How superfluous seem these quasars,
    pulsars, galaxies, black holes!
The sun, moon, earth, a sprinkling
    of stardust quite sufficiently declare
the grandeur of God. The rest simply
    underscore our finitude.

On a Berkshire morning
    my diamond ring in sunlight
reflects a tiny universe,
    expanding as my hand moves,
the Ptolemaic ring
    a playful planetarium.

In the cold of night,
    under the stars,
my ringed hand reaches for another.
    Together we survey the sky
with gratitude for
    the Star of Bethlehem.

I Do Not Come with Ease

I do not come with ease now
to the manger.

In earlier years
I caught the tinsel spirit,
cheered as gala lights festooned the streets.
I was the guileless shepherd in the fields
taken unaware by angels
singing peace, good news to all.

Today I follow wise men to the king,
who promises to come and worship, too.
Like them, I want to warn the Child
to flee, to find a different world
hospitable to innocence.

The strength of broken love prevails.
I join the wise men, shepherds, and dumb beasts
in painful praise
that God so loved
this world.

Anno Domini

A few minutes from Jerusalem
lies Bethlehem,
where street-Wise Men
haggle for souvenirs
in shops across the parking lot from
a huddle of churches
elbowing their altars
over the manger.

The manger! So unlike
our church-lawn crèche back home.
This low and smoky cave
enforces bowing of the knees
before the shelf of dirt
where God knows who was born.
Sheep and cattle shared this acrid space
alive with candles now
and wandering tourists,
who, ducking through the tunnel
to this humble room,
leave behind the incense, gold,
and vaulted altars
of quarrelsome tradition.

Here—in this dirt-simple void—
the issue must be joined
between humanity and God,
all tinsel, trees, and trappings
of two thousand holidays aside,
all incantations, vestments, hymns
suspended.

If God be born *here*
in this child,
no human birth disqualifies
as child of God.

Our modest crèche back home
may permutate details,
but limns
the mystery.

Christmas Past

Christmas baubles droop upon the bough,
as evergreen betrays its name indoors.

And cakes seem laden now
    with calories
instead of candied fruits and brandied nuts,
    ominously marked REDUCED
    in grocery bins.

The cheerful mystery of packages
    in virgin wrap
is now exposed beneath the drying tree:
    the woolen shirt with sleeves too short,
    the leather-fragrant wallet still uncreased,
    a well-selected book already paged,
    and fine-laced lingerie so cherished
        that next Christmas it will lie abed
        in tissue, yet unworn.

Carols, ringing with nostalgia and hope,
    soothing weary shoppers through the crowds,
now sound cloying or unutterably sad.

For Christmas, too, must pass.
    The diners lose
        anticipation once the turkey's carved,
        the bones turned into soup.
    The glow of glad goodwill grows cold
        as Yule logs turn to ash upon the hearth.

The yearly passage back to Bethlehem
    lies through Gethsemane,
    up Golgotha,
    and—unsuspecting—down Emmaus' road.

As eloquence must pause
    to gather thought,
and music needs the silence to shape sound,
so human spirit needs its fallow time,
    to yearn, to labor, to anticipate,
    then to grasp the Star and celebrate.

Why Must We Have a Cradled God?

Why must we have a cradled God,
    a pitiful, wailing, disabled God?
Why, when moon-striding, rocketing man
    flings his gauntlet across the span
    of universe with its unknown men,
must God be put in the manger again?

Because God wants us to know our birth:
    not children of stars or children of earth,
but—seeing the Parent in the Child,
    trusting and joyful and undefiled—
    children of love who inherited
the universe in the manger bed.

A Sonnet to Christmas Past

The trees lean wearily against the fence
    like sales clerks on their counters after dusk,
While banks urge Christmas savings one year hence
    and toward their hapless debtors act more brusque.
The city streets have lost their festive light,
    where greedy shoppers bargain or exchange
The gifts that just a week ago were bright
    with generosity that now seems strange.

So Christmas comes and goes without a trace?
    We seem too neon-blinded for the Star,
Unless we claim stigmata of God's grace
    by yearning for a Christmas we can't mar,
Remembering that Herod, Pilate tried
    to kill the Love that voluntarily died.

A Perennial Annual Word

Stumbling through the holidays
with forced rituals of joy
out the back door
of the old year,
we confront once again
our finitude.

> The new year
> (in a mild attack of optimism)
> is like gazing from the rocky cliffs of Crete
> > to the empty reaches of the sea,
> > its depths of shifting blue,
> > its silver froth,
> or, if you prefer, Nantucket.

Mostly, though,
the new year
is like waking under the same worn coverlet,
with the same gray January scene
outside the window as last year,
but—and this is why we humans
> pool our courage
> in contrived festival—
noting that the coverlet is a bit more worn,
the hands upon it more clearly veined and etched
with cumulative cares.

> Our annual event
> is stubbornly courageous.
> We can't ignore earth's daily pirouette,
> but why must we
> track her graceful do-si-do
> with the sun?
> We could have chosen Halley's Comet
> and bravely drunk champagne
> once in a lifetime!

A lifetime . . . "Aye, there's the rub."
However we may space the seconds,
we can't muffle the ticking clock.

In God's mercy
we enter the new year
with the strength of Christmas.
The Creator of this cosmic entropy
assures us that a lifetime
is just the beginning,
  that thirty-three arbitrary human years
  mark the heartbeat of eternal love
  preserving all creation.

▼

Refugee

Heavy with child,
this poor unmarried girl
came to my door,
almost too late.
I had no room she could afford;
I sent her to a nearby shed.
Her boyfriend, worried
and a bit confused,
watched over her
throughout the pains.
Sometimes these homeless folk
are gentle, too.
I saw the baby only once.
A crowd had gathered round,
curious, subdued.
He seemed an ordinary child,
but with no place
to lay his head.
I guess he'll be a refugee—
poor and full of grief.
I'm glad I had a bit of space
for them to use.
It seemed the human thing to do.

Noel for a Nuclear Age

When I attempt to contemplate
    the death of earth—
    the string of zeros
    that denotes the numbered dead:
    people "and much cattle"—
I only see a row of vacant eyes.

But I have seen a child at play
    in Leningrad, a target
    of our missiles
    in the wheat fields of the West.
    For such a numbered child
I daily pray and hope and work for peace.

Perhaps someone in Moscow saw
    a child at play in Central Park,
    target of a missile
    from the East and prays for peace.
    For in a child God births
the love to reconcile a dying world.

Slaughter of Innocence

A loving craftiness—and mercy—saved
    a child in Egypt from the pharaoh's fear
of Israelites, whose numbers gathered strength
    despite enslavement and the death of sons.
In turn, in time, the baby Moses saved
    his people from the pharaoh and his wrath.

A wise and wondrous warning spared a child
    in Israel from Herod's massacre.
His parents fled to Egypt with their son,
    while Herod's passion raged across the land.
In turn, in time, the baby Jesus saved
    all people who respond and walk God's path.

Today no Egypt shields our progeny,
    for earth itself, depleted at our hands,
may wreak unwitting vengeance on frail life.
    We warn of danger we ourselves have wrought.
In turn, in time, will children plunder, too,
    or save their habitat from nature's wrath?

▼

II

Parent and Child

▲

Birth Announcement

NAME: Timothy Donald Shriver
WEIGHT: 6 lbs. 3 oz.
LENGTH: 19 in.
BIRTH DATE: 8:27 P.M., Feb. 3, 1961

Statistics. Such bare bones
 on which to hang a human life!

"How long was labor?"
"Were you conscious through it all?"
"Did you hear the baby cry?"
"Did everything go well?"

Answers: Four hours. Yes-yes-yes.
 (But no one dares to ask The Question:
  Where did he come from and what does it mean?)

There are questions with no verbal answers . . .
 feelings which no words can echo . . .
  facts which can only be accepted.

Can the sum
 of even so brief a life
  be totaled?
Or the intensely alive
 excruciating moment of thrust
  be communicated?

 I was there, wide-eyed,
  dazzled by white lights, sanitary linens.
 My whole body listened, looked, strained,
  felt the holy urgency of that moment.
 But I did not see how or why
  he came to be our child.

We are creatures, not creators.
We can name, weigh, measure, note the hour, and—
 impelled by a drive
  beyond our own will and strength—
   produce a body.
But the biology lecture is inadequate
 in the delivery room.

16

Somehow—for some reason—he exists:
So, tremulously, we accept him
        as our child,
already knowing
        that he came from
            and still belongs
                to someone else.

▼

A Child's Debt

Your debt of copper coins
        is mine by legal right;
once they had been my gift
        before they were my due.

But when obedient fingers
        probe your narrow purse,
and copper turns to gold
        in your soft hand,

I yearn to cry out, "Stop!
        You needn't pay at all.
Here—you may have some more.
        Obedience is enough."

The ambiguity
        of God's just love constrains.
With gentle firmness I
        exact your debt.

A Prayer for Life's Seasons

Guide our years of childhood, Lord,
    so that we shall grow to be
    loving toward humanity.
Thank you for this precious world.
    Help us learn its history
    full of your great mystery.

Take the vigor of our youth.
    Give direction to its course,
    your own purpose to endorse.
Love us into loving truth.
    Lead us to its holy source.
    Bring us respite from remorse.

Hold us steady as we tread
    journeys of our middle years
    fraught with joys and cares and fears.
We, with hands and heart and head,
    glorify through deeds and cheers
    One who wipes away all tears.

Bless the waning of our days.
    If confusion clouds our sight,
    should disease our bodies blight,
Steer in gentle, calming ways
    faltering steps into the night,
    till the breaking forth of light.

This poem has been arranged by Alec Wyton to the hymn tune by Paul Heinlein (1626–1686).

Day Care—For Whom?

To the New Bern Avenue Day Care Center, Raleigh, North Carolina

Before your eager eyes
   one day I sat
and stroked my cello
   into throbbing song.
You danced and laughed
   and touched its vibrant chest.

The cello lured you
   into singing, too,
and like a waterfall
   your music flowed
and bubbled into joy
   around my feet.

A hundred friends
   have knocked upon your door
with little gifts
   of friendliness to share.
Like me, they left
   with more than they had brought—
endowed with fancy,
   mirth, delight and love.

Adulteration

Showers leave their reservoirs
    on glutted walks and lawns.
Children slosh in giant's boots
    their land of leprechauns.

But I—
    I mincing step to higher ground.

Lawns have gobbled up the woods,
    one tangle undefiled.
Children, spurning grass, explore
    the secrets of the wild.

But I—
    I tread the narrow concrete paths.

Caught by convention, trapped by taboo,
hobbled in heels and girdled in bone,
molded or withered, numbed, tamed or stale,
slowly I'm dying, or turning to stone.

On a Childlike Plane

So maturely in command aloft,
    on touching earth
the plane becomes a howling child
    waddling home
    to nuzzle into place
        among the suckling litter.
Nudged free, it lurches
    to the runway, thrusts,
    assumes nobility among the clouds,
dependence
    temporarily
        suspended.

▼

III
Dialogue

▲

Dialogue

You may
  read love letters aloud
      and no one snickers,
  put quotes around revered truth
      and sense no kinship with Servetus,
  blurt a new thought rough as cinder
      and see it polished to a gem,
  watch a theory, neat as well-made beds,
      be tousled and rumpled by lovers.

You may
  admit a festering deep within
      and let respectful questions probe the wound,
  detonate some person's hidden fuse
      and sweep debris together,
  expose your awful emptiness
      and be enriched,
  ask huge questions that engulf old answers
      and not despair.

For the search of two
      is better than
          the finding of one.

Eucharist

A friendly steaming coffee cup,
    between me and your vacant chair,
and conversation-rich dark bread
    sit mute: caloric, stimulant—
just body-stoking daily fuel
    for those dull absent hours.

There must be some communicant
    with whom to break this bread, or I
will choke upon my loneliness
    that clings like arid crusts. Perhaps
by listening to my mind's affairs
    I'll find companionship.

Suppose I listen soberly,
    acknowledging my emptiness.
I'll be receptive, open to
    the presence of the Lord of Bread
around whose table we both sit—
    wherever you may be.

Love, When You Have Gone Away

Time crouches on my shoulder
like a cat waiting to spring,
to come alive.

My living is provisional,
just "for the time being"—until
you arrive.

I am a letter torn in half,
words groping for completion
to contrive

a meaning from inchoate fragments,
An end to this long sentence.
I survive

the shallow breath of that hiatus.
Then—you fill my lungs with joy,
and I revive.

Airplane Landing

From my window in the sky
I see the world go whirling by:

Rivers wriggling to the sea,
Forests greening up at me,

Stripes and squares and polka dots
Of farms and trees and garden plots.

Fields and towns seem held in shape
By highways of adhesive tape.

One gay pattern I can see,
A carpet of community.

The nearer to the earth I go
The less that pattern seems to show.

Walls rise up and trees blot out
My patterned neighbors round about.

In my yard I look with guilt
At all the fences we have built.

Home Town

Viewed from a distant hill
this village can be blotted out
    by my thumbnail,
leaving an expanse
    of combed cornfields
    and empty pastures.

But as I walk its streets
    (I do not need to know their names,
    just "Mildred's corner lot" and
    the "brick banker's house
    across from Dr. Stowe's")
I am enclosed
by neighbors.

Some streets I never travel to their end,
but stop short,
before the houses give out.
Just once I walked beyond,
to what had always looked to be a dropping-off place—
my private mystery—
and found Ver Ploeg's deep pasture;
behind the fence his lazy horse
gazed down the village street
back of me.
I turned quickly toward the square,
disquieted by loss,
though common sense had told me long ago
the farm was there.

Houses straggle out the edges of the town
like unkempt hair that strays beneath a cap,
yet even they are bound in neighborhood
    around the square.

Years ago I crossed that distant hill
and left my village far behind,
    but I never raised my thumb
    to banish it,
    for I too am a straggler
    bound to the village square.

Set the Table for Our Neighbors

Set the table for our neighbors.
Lay before them bread and wine.
Make a place for friends and strangers.
Offer gifts of grain and vine.

Join us at this holy table
Where the savior is our host.
Feast upon his love and mercy.
Make obedience your toast.

Emptied now of fear and tension,
Full of hope, of love and grace,
We, in gratitude and silence,
Bow in prayer before his face.

Gather close to one another.
Strengthened by this sacred meal,
We receive Christ's holy presence
And, for others, make him real.

This poem has been set to music in an original hymn tune by John Weaver.

A Sickness of the Ill

Eyes listen, attentive to
    the secret messages within.

My body, self-enclosed,
    recycles fear,
    its sensors nagging
        wayward, broken parts.

A claustrophobic stillness
    haunts my mind,
    the world shrunk
        to an epidermal layer
        enclosing my bruised self.

(A patient—oh so patiently—
    takes inventory hour by hour!)

Cradled in a sickbed,
    I drowse
    in my own womb.

I must strangle this sweet narcissism
    with my own hands,
        clasping them with neighbors,
        for to love is health.

Neighbors

For years I watched you work your yard,
    as I my farm;
but recently another cuts your grass
    while you lean on a cane
        and, lately, two.
So now you sit on wheels.
I know deep trouble bends your knees.

Eight years I've been your neighbor
    and we've never shared our names.
You are professor; I, a janitor
    and farmer in a field outside our town.

No matter that my tongue
    is thickened by strange words
        and salted by my Dutch.
We hear beyond the sounds.

I am a Christian man, so it's a shame
    that just my waving hand
        has spoken for eight years
          of living close.

Today I cannot simply wave
    as you sit bent upon those wheels,
for broken speech no longer blocks
    the offer of my healthy arms
        to serve your need.

God grant that soon
    we may be neighbors
        in our joy
          as in our suffering.

A Reflection on Marriage

I gaze into your smiling eyes
    and see myself reflected there.
I know you see your image
    in the darkness of my eyes—
        "deep calling unto deep"
      in infinite reflection.

Our eyes bespeak the glory of our love—
    each profoundly dwelling
      in the other;
    each identifying self
      through lenses of the other;
    each warmed and strengthened
      by the vibrancy received.

Never break that gaze, my love,
    or I shall perish
    in the half-life
    of my empty eyes.

Fill Us with Vision

With the sinews of the Spirit
    we shall bind our brokenness.
With the warm blood of forgiveness
    we shall learn to live as one.

Refrain: Fill us with vision,
          Fill us with vision,
          Fill us with vision and hope
              for our time.
          Give us strength,
          Teach us love,
          Bring us joy in our unity.
          Fill us with vision and hope
              for our time.

Now disarming grace shall guide us
    toward a future ripe with hope,
Where tomorrow's children flourish
    on the fruits of righteous peace.

We shall tell our cherished stories,
    share our pilgrim sacred lore,
Meet our savior in each other
    and the strangers on our way.

We must till our trampled garden,
    probe earth's mysteries with awe,
Use our skills to serve creation
    and God's human family.

Listen to God's holy silence
    throbbing with the power of love.
Pray in cadence with God's children
    faithfully living the Holy Word.

Cleanse the purpose of our nation.
    Be a partner of God's will.
Let the power of resurrection
    flow through us into the world.

This may be sung as a hymn to the tune of "Waltzing Matilda" in stately tempo. It
is a verse version of the National Council of the Churches of Christ in the U.S.A.'s
Ecumenical Agenda for the 1980s.

Who Are We?

We are Christ's broken body,
    a divided household,
        a tangle of branches on the true vine,
          but still we *are* the Church.

Dare we hope the hope
    to which we have been called?
        To grow up in every way
          into him who is the head—

Into Christ, from whom the body,
    rightly joined and knit together,
        grows through due activity
          and upbuilds itself in love?

Claire's Hands

Claire's hands embrace the air,
    containing dreams.
Molding, shaping, sculpting them,
    the artist in her works
until her hope is visible.

Fingers trace the blur of words
    upon a page and come to rest
upon essential thoughts or
    tap the word most unfelicitous.

Strong and blunt, her cryptic pen
    conveys a firm resolve.
Her forceful, unembroidered notes
    record the rainfall of a hundred
cloudy conversations.

She probes at problems tangled
    like a ball of gathered thread,
until the threads begin to loosen
    under her persistent tug.

Sometimes the crises mount
    like jackstraws on her desk.
With mind and hand and heart
    allied, she extricates
the straws most needing care.

Hands that raise a glass to joy,
    that sparingly caress except in truth,
are restless in the folds of prayer
    but open wide in boundless praise.

Her Amos-God prefers
    the active tense of prayer.

A Politic Proposal

If you are the Christ,
let's elect you king!
    Plenty in this Roman world
    needs setting right.
With you in charge our troubles disappear:
    the weak made strong,
    the proud brought low,
    the land restored
    to our control.

Come on, Lord.
We'll join your monarchy
and pay you proper court.
    Just say the word
    and our campaign begins.
With God on our side,
your victory is sure.

What do you mean, Lord,
that's not your style?
    If you prefer,
    take on the *world*.
    Then you can rule us all.
God would like that, too.

I'm disappointed in you, Lord.
What use is "a kingdom
    not of this world"?
With all your clout,
your heavenly connections,
    you could pull off
    a landslide.
What, me?
    You expect *me*
    to change the world?

I'm sorry, Jesus.
We could have made a great team.

But I've got other prospects anyway.
I know another crowd
····so eager for my help
······they've offered
··········thirty pieces
············of silver.

▼

The People

We came to hear the President,
····this stranger and I.
He sat squat in front of me,
····right full cheek brushing
····my presidential view.

Across that cheek bone spread
····a purplish scar.
Had birth been cruel—or was
····tragedy tattooed
····upon his face?

We heard the words: honor, loyalty,
····the people—and I looked
at "the people" in front of me:
····nondescript brown suit, balding head,
····flushed neck, the scar.

He glanced no self-disclosure.
····Indeed, he never saw me.
But when I think of presidents
····and people,
····I recall him;

For in some deeply human sense
····we were there together.

▼

IV
Abysses and Alienations

▲

A Day at Grand Canyon

I stand at the canyon rim
    as ridges recede
        apparently in infinite regress,
        growing fainter like an echo
            of an echo
            of an echo.

Voices drop into a hush
    as sunfire ignites the rim,
        spreading downward in silent
        conflagration. Even the wind
            holds its breath, as daily ritual fire
            passes crest to crest.

Scoured by wind and wet
    to an integrity of wrinkles,
        Mother Earth reveals herself
        in brilliant sun, unadorned
            by flattery of flower
            or shielding tree.

No coquetry diverts the eye.
    Two billion years of grinding time
        unblinkingly display
        the dignity
            and grandeur
            of the gloriously old.

No maternal warmth invites me
    to this jagged barren womb.
        I am alien, an intruder.
        Cold heat, raw wind and lashing torrents
            show no mercy,
            no cognition.

I stammer
    like a child before
        this calm, imperious presence,
        no frame of words sufficient
            to enclose these vast perimeters
            of space and time.

Slowly the sun withdraws,
    leaving cool shadows on seared rock.
        Far below, the river continues
        its remote tantrum,
            having worn its stubborn way
            for centuries.

The ritual fires climb again the canyon rim,
    extinguished one by one
        from peak to higher peak
        as the sun bows and canyon softens
            before the wise silence
            of night.
                I, too, kneel.

▼

Beyond, the Stars . . .

Beyond, the stars are fleeing from our eyes.
Our heavy lenses point in sharp pursuit.
Extensions of ourselves, they scan the skies
while spinning, hurtling an untraveled route.
Though dusty space throws sand into our sight,
our calculations blindly probe until
we read stale news from dimly blinking light,
confirming cosmic systems vaster still.
Pursuers of the truth, the human race
reveals the grandeur given it to find.
Yet we are not quite lost in astral space;
the universe we map within our mind.
    Although such knowledge decimates conceit,
    the very knowing is itself a feat.

Solar Plexus
March 7, 1970

Inexorably swift the moon
races to its rendezvous:
unerring conjunction, calculated,
not transistorized, by humans who—
despite their lenses, sextants, armillaries—
battle within
the terror of primeval life;
    when birds converse nervously in twilit trees
    frogs protest the purple air
    flowers tremble in the silence
    roosters proclaim a maverick dawn
    herds lumber homeward under wild stars
and the chill of separation
strikes cold in the heart.

Ripples of shadows
like shock waves of cosmic collision
transmit a terrible awe.

Venus and Mercury guard the vacant-faced, fiery Medusa
before whose image we become stone-blind,
immobile in the anxiety of dependence.

Oblivious, the moon pursues its rounds
as birds, frogs, flowers, beasts and we
exult in solar warmth again.

We return to our calculus, sextant, telescopes,
recording all readings
    except our heartbeat.

Storm Warning

Like a dance of veils,
    white upon deep blue,
thin wisps of cloud
    conjure silently,
expanding—out of nothing—
    into grotesque forms.

A cancer sickening the sky,
    these foreboding clouds—
as insubstantial as my nameless fears—
    tower, nonetheless,
until with sudden chill
    they blot out the sun.

My world is momentarily gray.
    Then, stealthily, the clouds glide on,
and I am wrapped in warmth,
    grateful for the constancy of sun
but hoarding strength
    for shadows yet to come.

Plantation

Spanish moss
silently drops its ragged curtain
over the waning years
of heroic water oaks.

Beyond the avenue of pines
white columns stolidly uphold
the dignity of human struggle
against encroaching swamp.

A century of human history rests
on squat brick pedestals.

Inside thick walls
the swamp seeps insidiously
with rot, rust, web and mildew.

Outside, nut grass and strangling vines
are hacked and ripped repeatedly
to carve a clearing.

The swamp is not the victor.
Yet, vulturelike, it awaits
        the unraveling of frail family ties,
        the dwindling of fortune,
        or rush of cars
            down other avenues.

Benefice

My deed of transfer claims I own
    twelve thousand squares of Carolina clay.
How many cubits deep: until the hot rock melts
    and intermixes with my neighbor's?
How many cubits high: until the taunting birds
    can scarcely tilt against my sky?

Illiterate nature disdains my title duly traced:
    Stray dogs, cats, squirrels, birds,
        insects, worms and snakes
        trespass brazenly upon my lawn.
    My tall oak's revolving shade,
        obedient only to the sun,
        cools first my neighbor.
    Lemon lilies nod from side to side
        down the border of my lawn,
        greeting all who pass.
    Our maple wings its seeds across the avenue,
        while dandelions parachute upon my lawn
        from distant launching pads.
    Violets and ferns cheerfully proliferate
        through rigid fences,
        while ivy climbs the highest walls.

I brandish my papers helplessly
    at the hailstorm,
    the high wind,
    the rain that washes topsoil down the hill.
For while the tenant farmer's field
    is regal with Queen Anne's lace,
both his elm and mine, ravished by disease
    stalking the land from east to west,
    are stark skeletons clawing at the sky.
And the hidden waters rush
    beneath our soil
    to an undeeded sea.

How many cubits do I own?
I have just squatter's rights,
    a temporary loan,
    and my title is:
        Vassal.

Wildacres

Relaxing on your porch throne,
 coffee mugs steaming the cool night air,
we hold court over the passing day:

> . . . the snake thief who emerged
> through the deck boards
>   to snatch a gasping fish

> . . . the yellowhammer's avarice
> for green-painted houses

> . . . snuffling deer who roam the hills

> . . . gawky adolescent Christmas trees,
> awaiting the pruning discipline
>   of a few more years

> . . . shy strawberries, blushing
> through ragged leaves

> . . . and always the heavy rim of hills,
> boiling up clouds
>   throughout the day.

In gratitude we watch the day
 fade quietly into the stars.

You "own" this mountain,
but you would agree
Wildacres is a democracy
with nature holding a decisive vote.

Lord of the Dance
1970 Solar Eclipse

With silent pirouette
the ballet of the spheres
performs a cosmic choreography:

> As lights dim
> before a hushed, awed crowd,
> the lunar pygmy smoothly slips
> the flaming giant on his back.

> Still racing, gliding noiselessly,
> without a pause, a gasp,
> the pygmy dances on alone.
> The giant beams.

Lights blaze.
The crowd murmurs,
shouts approval to
the Lord of the Dance.

Cosmic Conundrum

When the last dish was put away
    and Mother's apron hung upon its nail,
we gathered in the yard to glimpse the sky
    and watch the sun pull back its fading light.

Slowly the stars emerged, shy actors
    on the universal stage, where we, too,
are both audience and cast—and dance
    in imperceptible ballet.

Sensing the evening's existential chill,
    I nestled on my father's ample lap,
relaxed against his reassuring chest,
    and heard the rumble of his calming voice

as he described Orion's stride above,
    or calculated distances of light
emitted by our neighbor Betelgeuse,
    or spoke respectfully of galaxies.

He talked of great red giants and white dwarfs,
    of flaring sunspots and a meteor's death,
and of the secret sorcery of the moon
    that tugs the tidal waters of the sea.

As we both aged in knowledge cosmically,
    he added quasars, pulsars, nebulae,
and "black holes" where the heavy stars collapsed,
    or questions about life on other worlds.

Despite expansions of my canopy,
    I felt at home within its awesome space.
Guided by my father's certainty
    the heavens meant not to intimidate

but simply be: a statement of "what is
    and ever more shall be"; a mystery,
a puzzle; hints among that vast debris
    for creatures loved to life to contemplate.

Tomatoes

Past our sentinel tomatoes
    tramp dusty, bare brown feet.
Below the hill—
    "Out of sight,
    out of mind"—
huddle dusty, bare brown huts.

An odd parade, these neighbors:
    old little girls in tired cottons,
rummage-sale mothers
    withered and bony,
    broken-arched and heavy,
dragging tired, dusty brown feet home.

"You got mighty nice 'maters!"
    "I sure could use some 'maters. . . . "
Why do I hesitate
    to hand out tomatoes,
    to dole out tomatoes,
when I've more than enough for my own?

Perhaps it is that I know
    pride has been broken—
just for tomatoes.
    Can my hands,
    my white hands,
heal my neighbors' hurt . . . with tomatoes?

Berry Boy

Peeking through my screen,
a briar-thin boy with purpled hands
stands clasping a battered berry pail.

"Blackberries, ma'am?
Forty cent a quart."

That compressed plural,
typical economy of the poor,
softens his demand.

Kneeling together, we admire
the glistening berries. Four hands—
both pairs colored with juice—
heap blackberries into my white bowl.

We smile, and, thinking to be kind,
I say, "How nice they are.
Where did you pick them?"

The white smile closes on his dark face.
Eyes dull, wary and distant,
he snatches his pail, murmurs,
"By the tracks,"
and he is gone.

Lavish nature has supplied this public welfare,
with no case records, no questions,
just free berries for patient fingers.

"Blackberries are for black hands,"
he does not dare to say.

Dark Glasses

Black brother,
why do you walk in purdah
with your veiled dark eyes?

Is the glare of this white world
so painful you must blacken it
to feel at ease?

Or is a fierceness
smoldering in your eyes
that you would—for the moment—
spare me?

From which direction
flares the blinding heat:
From both?
(Are glasses, then, an insulating screen
to keep us cool?)

I cannot really see you
I complain to those closed doors
into yourself.

From enigmatic depths
comes your reply:
"You haven't really seen me
for a hundred years."

City of Mourning

Over Atlanta
a weeping sky
sags like canvas
upheld by the city's concrete towers,
a vast tent of mourning.

A carpet of green trees
displays Atlanta's wise conservancy.
But for this stricken city,
ribbons of incongruous green
signal death.

Sin-sick hands
strangle the future
from throats of black youth,
their grotesque act
a mockery
of the city "too busy to hate."

That fierce and holy love for
        bone of one's bone,
        flesh of one's flesh
endures and purifies,
while hatred, when exposed,
        shrivels
        into trite obscenity.

The anguish of a mother's "Why?"
        overwhelms reply.
If evil be unmasked,
        mystery will remain.

Mourners,
        gathered in a global wake
        beneath this sacred canopy,
kneel in dreadful grief,
companioned by a God
        who also gave a child
                to violence.

The Development of Ahmadu

We got him first as houseboy, Ahmadu,
    his eyes like cameras recording all,
    and ears that listened most when least alert,

But soon we dubbed him Bob, because he learned
    our western ways so eagerly and well.
Of course we took his broom and gave him books,
    then sent him from his village to a school,
    where appetite outgrew the local lore.

We brought him to the States, and by degrees
    he found his place: his job, his wife, his home.
Bob seldom wrote his parents (what's to write?)
    and entertained his friends with memories
        of primitive traditions, rites, taboos,
        and weird concoctions hunger drives men to.

We'd hoped he might return to save his race,
    but then, if in his shoes, what would we do?
It is a shame his brother, smarter still,
    won't come to be developed like him, too.

Tribal Development

My people in the village feared for me
>when I began to speak in strangers' tongues
>and uttered prayers our fathers never prayed.

They claimed the uniform I wore at school
>had bleached me white beneath the well-stitched cloth,
>and for an agony of months I wished it so.

Ashamed of tribal ways and poverty,
>I envied men so nonchalantly rich
>and self-assured in their technologies.

But when I knew their God was my God too,
>I slowly learned to love myself again,
>to cherish village dust between my toes.

A connoisseur of cultures now am I,
>not clinging to or giving up my own,
>but shaping, as God wills, the human tribe.

To a Masai University Student

Masai,
you stalk three thousand years:
from Tanzania's smoked dung hut
to Kenya's hoteled streets,
where windows boast
your mother's beaded wares
as curios to lure
the stranger's purse.

The same black hand
that proudly demonstrates
your test of manhood
    (how, with heavy knotted stick
    and left arm sheathed in cloth,
    you faced alone the lion,
    thrust the stick between his jaws,
    then jabbed your spear
    into his heart
    and breathed the blood-salt air—a man!)
now sketches boldly, too,
the buildings you will engineer
for all your tribe.

Your hand drops limp, Masai,
as you confess your need
for sheets and mattress now,
and windows in your room—
no more the straw bed
hollowed by the calves
in smoky darkness.

Fearless and agile,
you leapt three thousand years.
Your tribesmen taunt.
But some young man,
intrigued by aeons in your eyes,
may dare the chasm, too.

Kinshasha Ivory Market
(Zaire)

Crouched, pacing, kneeling,
ready to spring,
the Congo traders ambush
the rich Americans, the rich Europeans,
    the camera-laden.

        You know fetish?
        Elephant hair—strong magic.
        Fifty makuta for fetish, madame.
        Forty? Will you buy for forty?

Casually spread upon the ground
lie varied treasures:
ivory, malachite, ebony, gold—
gaudy tropic scenes and vibrant skillful art
beside the elephant ear bag,
the snakeskin belt,
the amulet of feathers.

        Pardon, les peintures, madame,
          s'il vous plaît.
        Fine painting!
          Qu'est-ce que vous donnez?

Behind each offering a wary artisan,
tapping, fondling, waving
his favored piece,
pierces the tourist with his eye.

        Come on, ten dollars.
        Five zaire, only five.
        For you, four-fifty makuta.
        Just for you.

Three, four, five persistent hawkers
thrust dark hands into my face;
scorning my bewilderment,
they press their goods against my hand.

What will you give me?
It is yours. Name it.
Here. This snakeskin wallet.
What will you give?

The Congolese, with sharp experienced eyes,
take my measure,
probe for weakness,
weigh my purse,
override my protest,
boldly push their claims.

For you, little lady.
Ten zaire.
For you I make it ten.
You like this malachite?
Ah, the ivory. Very good work.
But cheap, so cheap.

Suddenly no longer in the market,
I see a slave block
in New Orleans
a hundred years ago.
The insolent eyes, bold hands,
demanding tones—are mine!

Non, merci, monsieur!
Pardon!
Pardon!

The Bull Leapers of Knossos

Against a mariner's blue sky
tall cypresses
engage within themselves
in mute debate—
dark green arms and heads
gesticulate, nodding,
dancing free.
On silent cue
they suddenly compose themselves
into consensual wands
that magically enliven
this labyrinth of rocks.

Patiently
dusting away the years,
lovers of the past
coax Minos' palace
from the dead.
They secure tottery old stones,
puzzle each room's use,
mend storage jars,
infer the unseen from the seen
in maddeningly marred mosaics.

Proud-bosomed fresco maidens turn
their sloe-eyed profiles toward
the portico
among whose columns the queen goddess
walked.
Blue dolphins,
playful as today's cartoons,
frolic on her chamber wall.

Such frescoes speak to us,
decoded with a passionate fidelity,
each fleck of paint or stone
a Cretan word.

Most eloquent of all,
the bull dancers of Knossos
lithely leap upon the bull's broad back,
a fading fresco frozen
in a brazen taunt
at death.

Their agile courage
graces these dim walls,
a testament to life.
Bull dancers of today
must brave the beast
within themselves,
or leap a fungus cloud
of deadly dust.

Generation Gap

An avalanche
of hungry mountain poor
   descended to the mills,
      their faces cleft,
         eroded as the slopes
         they left behind,
            bronzed as sun-baked crags
            and lit by fierce, determined eyes
            that glinted waterfalls.

They hear their mountain tunes
of wind and rain and birds
   transposed into the hum
      of whirring spindles,
      slapping shuttles,
      singing threads,
         as doors slide shut.

The fiber hothouse,
   humid, stale, and huge,
      employs a team of gardeners
         for each slim strand.

While woven rolls
 of springtime flowers
    flourish on the looms,
workers breathe
 a sterile pollen,
    dusting lungs with death.

When whistles shriek,
 the workers shuffle,
    pale and weak-eyed
       into light,
like insects startled
 by a lifted stone.

They stretch and numbly
 shake monotony
by seeking frantic joy,
 or solace in hereafter's hope.

But mountain children
  have a present hope.
They see their parents' wretched bodies,
  prematurely aged,
and vow to ride their meager heritance
  away from upland slopes,
    away from mills.

Auction Trespassers

Exposed in the bright sun lie
    love-stained mattresses
        with listless springs;
  a brass-bound trunk
      gaping memories
      and dead treasure:
  a wine-colored velvet gown,
      high-buttoned vests,
      and mildewed lace,
mocked by the wash-and-wear crowd.

Guffaws greet a bulbous lamp.
A secondhand dealer,
    an old pro,
    nods at a box of china,
chancing an antique.
"Slim pickings today,"
    he mutters.

Someone "in the country"
    bids on a pasteboard box
    (a gentleman's gamble)
as the auctioneer hints
    at diamonds
    in the trash.

A presence inhabits the couch,
    hollowing its cushions
    and greasing its arms,
disturbing in its ragged dignity.

Looters, adventurers,
the orderly crowd
    in decent greed
strips bare a private past.

Dar es Salaam

Like Helen
  you have launched a thousand ships
  and lured each roving Paris
    with your smile of dazzling sand
     and languid palms.

At dusk
  you are a lovely blushing maid,
  bejeweled by the suitors
   lying, restless, near your shore,
  perfumed by tropic blooms that tremble
   gently on your breast,
  and softened by the flattery
  of mauve cosmetic glow.

But when
  the veils of morning mist are swept
   into the sea,
  a harsh white tropic sun stares, merciless,
   upon your aging face:
    each cruel shadow sharp and withering,
    mildew and mottled paint exposed by glare,
    and slimy seaweed hair limply afloat
    amid the flotsam of a thousand loves.
  Decay now subtly taints
   the fragrance at your throat
  and jewel lights extinguish with the dawn.

Again
  as twilight works its purple charm,
  Dar es Salaam plays Helen-by-the-Sea,
   and I, enamored Paris, quite forgive
   the daylight glimpse
    of your debauchery.

▼

V

Moments of Grace

▲

The Spirit of 34th Street

Doors opened with a silent scream,
    like photographs of anguish;
    the subway paused, shed cargo
        and raged on.

She lurched aboard,
    sagged into a vacant seat,
    frail weight of her gray years
        hunched with cold.

Numb fingers plucked at rags,
    drawn close against raw misery.
    Knuckles, cracked and swollen white,
        clutched into a plea for warmth.

He, dark and lithe,
    swung down the aisle,
    taut jeans dancing
        rhythmically.

With Latin grace
    he, sidling past
    her patient form,
        in one smooth gesture

disappeared through subway doors,
    leaving in her lap,
    like folded dove wings,
        his black leather gloves.

A Collision of Cups

Submissive to the thunder of the rails,
the riders rest their eyes unfocused
    on the subway floor,
    refusing the assault of insolent graffiti
    that taunt their alien and alienating scrawl
    everywhere but underfoot.

As doors slide open, bawling, then muffling the subway's roar,
a blind man feels the aisle with his feet,
    extending in his hand
    a cup of meager gratitude.
Wary passengers cast their good eyes
    upon that cup,
    but no one moves to fill it.

From opposing doors another tinkling symbol clangs;
a robust youth, lacking only legs,
    lurches down the aisle,
    his cup overflowing
    from obvious need.

The captive crowd, responding to his smile
And outstretched hand,
    tenses for the pending shoot-out
    of drawn cups.

Sensing the hulk—but not the crutches—before him,
the blind man shakes his cup.
Shifting his weight upon one crutch,
the boy plucks a coin
    from his own cup
    and drops it in the other.

Like loaves and fishes
the coins multiply
as passengers, abashed,
fill the blind man's cup.
    He moves slowly on,
    baffled by grace.

Unleavened Bread

Despite averted eyes I saw
his scraggy frame lean forward
in the pew as
the sacrament approached.

His weathered head nested
in a scarf of faded plaid
wound twice around his neck,
the one concession of his garb
to winter's taunts.
A cardboard box—his vagrant's home—
lay on the pillowed pew.

Jacket seams agape,
his arm stretched trembling
toward the bread.
He scooped a swath of matzo
in his hand
once, then twice
as it passed by again.

Greedily he stuffed God
to his mouth in haste,
as though he, too, must pack
provisions for a promised land
without the leavening of grace.

Lest his eagerness be misconstrued,
he shunned the wine,
dismissing murmurs
of Christ's blessing
with a shrug.

Accustomed as he was
to heed the transient's fear
of trespassing,
he chose to feast
on crumbs.

The Thief on the Crosswalk

Sprinting noiselessly
behind my back,
he grabbed my leather purse
  but caught hold of my life,
    wrenching loose its grip on confidence,
      toppling my body,
      face flat against
      the gritty truth of pavement,
      arm outstretched
      in forced farewell
      to things held dear.

His swift, crude surgery
excised the plastic cards
that reassure computers—
a fragile chain of numbers
that constitute the social DNA
of my genetic code.

    He furthermore exposed
    my naive protective claim
    to be exempt from violence
    on the premise that
    meaning well bodes well.

Gone, too, the coin and keys that honor
and legitimate belonging.
So instantly am I a refugee,
the world's welcome suddenly
grown cold.

Left with no money, pride, or place,
I walk these alien streets
and wonder
if the thief was running
from such destitution, too.

Christ forgave thieves
I reluctantly recall—
and the slow healing begins.

Tales of India

An ambush waits at corners
on Bombay's avenues:

> a vendor dangling
>   agate necklaces
> thrusts his gaunt arm
>   through our window's gap,
> withdrawing only as the car moves on

> a blind child hears the engine pause,
>   taps his imperious need
> upon our pane and rolls his eyes
>   so we must see
> the moist red pulp behind his lids

> another rubs his elbow stump
>   across the glass
> while sister pulls her face
>   into a piteous mask,
> competing with a crutch tip
>   pounding on the other door
> and cries of "Baksheesh!"
>   from the legless one.

We roll our windows high,
lower our eyes,
purse held firm
> by tales of children's butchery,
> maimed as merchandise for mercy—
>   thus mercy made
>   accomplice to brutality.

One night we ride with windows down
to catch the balmy breezes from the bay.
    A jaunty urchin greets us as we stop.
    Laughing, he throws a blossom in my lap.
        "I have no rupees with me" (which is true),
        I say and hold the flower out to him.
    He grins and shakes his head.
    We parry smiles until
        the light has changed and I, outdone,
        let go the lovely bloom.
In one quick swoop he rescues it
        and tosses it again upon my lap,
        then, smiling, darts away.

Ashamed, I dare not touch the gift
or share in its exotic loveliness,
      so unprepared am I
          for grace.

Holiness Has Wings

The unborn hopes
    of diligent maternal wings
    lay cooling on the window ledge.
Constancy had failed
    to halt a sad, mysterious curdling
    of two pigeon eggs.

Vivification overdue,
    both parents hunched upon the rail, their
    earnest bustling stilled to a portentous calm.
In gray despair
    they sat respectfully before
    the two calcific tombs.

Behind their dirgeful grief
    a gathering of birds descended to the trees and
    roosted in a silent requiem.
Their rite fulfilled,
    the mass of pigeon mourners
    solemnly withdrew

in wondrous mimicry
    of sentient human awe
    before Eternity
and evidence
    that holiness
    has wings.

Safari Tableau

Panting in the tall grass
three satiated lions lie at peace,
    remnants of a bloody feast
    of wildebeest among them.

Discreetly distant, vultures
huddle patiently in solemn groups
       like poor relations waiting
       for the reading of a will.

A silent herd of wildebeest
soberly attends its paschal lamb
    whose death assures a day of grace
    at the water hole.

An observer is prepared for violence,
not this orderly acceptance
    that all creatures must be fed,
       each taking his turn around the table
       or on it.

Consider the Pansies

Pansies
barely lift
their pensive faces
from the soil.

Soft and bright,
they congregate,
intimately warm.

No one places pansies
in imposing floral sprays.
They charm calm corners,
cling to edges
of a yard.

Pansies cease to bloom
if, with velvet eyes,
they fail to tempt
admirers' touch.

Gregarious
and generous,
they give themselves away
and flourish.

Horticultural Hortation

"Talk to your houseplants.
Let pleasant tones nourish them
    like dark warm soil
    or invigorating rain.

"Let them dance to Mozart
    and to Mendelssohn,
    tremble with Sibelius,
    pendulate with Bach.

"But shelter them from noise—
harsh, pounding, shrill, and loud,
for growing things need gentle sounds,
    caresses from the air."

        Such advice seems odd to me,
        so used am I to treating plants
        like ornaments, or backdrop
        to my own life's needs.

        But leaves' stomata waft aroma
        to enrich and purify the vapid air—
        reason enough to mumble clumsy thanks
        should houseplants need appreciation, too.

Atomic Harvest
1969

When the mushroom cloud
loosed its death spores
of black rain upon
the seared soil,
and parched seeds drank
in desperate need,
did flowers bloom again
in Hiroshima?

    Yes! the books exulted.
    Out of the rocks
    ancient dormant seeds
    awoke,
    challenged by the radiant flash
    of our destructive will,
    and blossomed.

Twenty-four years passed.
Then with believing eyes
I saw
the city resurrected.

    While guitars strummed
    and young feet danced,
    into my tainted hands
    a long-haired Hiroshima maid
    gently laid
    a flower.

Musings on an Honorary Degree

Have I been hood-winked?
Should I be mortarfied?
Or am I a Robing Hood
    with diplomatic immunity
        until the Final Exam,
when I'll discover
    with certainty
        whether one can
           become honorable
           by degrees?

▼

VI
Finitude

▲

Tape Message

A disembodied voice
　　　traced upon a tape
pulses through the room,

so tenuous its touch
　　　of life with other lives
as wheels are slowly wound

that words can choke and die
　　　before our startled ears
when power executes.

A "pacemaker" machine
　　　that kills the heart of speech,
it stops. We sit alone.

Terminal Illness

A restlessness
pervades this space
oddly called a "terminal,"
although it's not a journey's end.
    We are all
passing through,
rushing to wait,
waiting to rush,
time attentively wasted.
While the mind lingers,
imagination flies ahead.

Nothing is quite real
except the luggage.

At the departure gate
words die, spent of meaning,
while new arrivals greet
like segments of torn dollar bills
being matched,
finding value in relationship.

Stand-up fast-food bars
and stalls marked "duty free"
underscore our transience
and the separation
of our togetherness.
Having someplace else to go
keeps us alive.

Autumnal Leave-taking

Leaves have burned to ash upon the trees.
A gust of wind will scatter their remains,
as tribute to a summer harvested,
contributing to harvests germinant.

Restless with the selflessness of leaves,
we yearn to place our past upon the soil
in concrete, indestructible display
instead of nourishing a distant dream
posterity may till, perhaps to reap.

Sabbatical Finitude

We first notice a telltale spotting of red,
    symptom of the death of leaves,
when the pond no longer beckons for a swim.

The woods creak and groan like gossips comparing
    aches, after the leaves are shed.
A touch of gray in harvest gold shows in the sky.

Soon the sky wears lavender with lace of trees,
    as wild December turkeys strut
like flocks of successful postelection politicians.

Indoors, the length of unread books shortens smugly
    as piles of paper rise. But the forest stays
intractably uncleared, though feverishly hacked.

The flush of Christmas joy contends with a chill
    proleptic mourning, akin to Christmas wreaths,
which for the resurrected babe are crepe and crown.

Some books remain unread, poetry stillborn, a manuscript
    in travail, jaunts no longer planned, recipes
unsavored, love urgent still.

We drain the water pipes, let ashes cool,
    pack the perishables, load the car. We return
more alive and more aware of death.

Pity the Water Oak

Pity the water oak,
whose green fingers
yellow gracelessly
    into brown claws.

They die
in decayed old age.

When sap stiffens
in hardy maples,
their hands splay forth
    triumphant beauty.

They lie,
an ornament upon the ground.

Lord, is it too much
for me to ask
a maple's death?

Harvest

My days blossom

as a garden
through which I scamper,
plucking flowers
joyfully,

stuffing them
into a treasure box
of memory
unpressed, unsorted.

Someday my palsied

homebound hand
will search that box
for solace.

I will find

brown withered blooms,
crumbling into dust
within my palm.

But even shriveled petals

waft a fragrance
that evokes

our afternoon one autumn,
as we knelt upon dark sand

and sifted pebbles
through our fingertips,

in search
of a carnelian.

Retirement

His step had slowed,
    feet plodding through a silt of years.
His mind, aware of now,
    double-exposed it with the past.

Committees met, shook heads and hands,
    and gave him to his past—
the dead past.
    And so he died.

Nursing Home

Sinking, sinking within her chair arms,
she sits alone,
     absorbing another day
     into her shrunken frame.

Her hands smooth and pluck,
fold and crease,
     conditioned by long days
     of household toil.

At visiting hours
we almost tiptoe to her chair,
     afraid to disrupt
     her private peace.

She slightly turns and smiles,
but the disturbing thrust
     of a familiar face
     is so tauntingly elusive

that her own face
collapses in despair
     over a loss too profound
     to be recalled,

a loneliness suddenly grieved.
She speaks,
     scattering her thoughts
     like sparrows.

Her words are a kaleidoscope
of sound, images that break
     into new images,
     a continuity of discontinuities.

We pat her restless hands,
caress her doll-sized form,
     and gently leave her leaning,
     exhausted, in the everlasting arms.

Here, Child, a Lily

With one bright smile you capture
    the tiger in your hand,
and mirror its wild rapture—
    then toss it in the sand.

I retrieve the bloom untamed.
    Its petals burn though bruised;
momentarily time's redeemed,
    so prodigally used.

For I, half spent, must like this flower
    die when my day is through,
grateful for every beauty-filled hour.
    Come, child—look again, too.

The Fighter

Crane poised,
the heavy wrecking ball
swung hard
against the concrete wall,
swung, crashed,
and swung again.

One man,
concave from eighty years'
harsh blows,
grinned slyly to his peers,
laughed, coughed,
and laughed again.

"I poured that concrete fifty years ago
and saw the ribs of steel beneath her skin.
They'll lose some bucks on her," he prophesied,
"and brag they downed a fighter when she's died."

For days
the wall did not relent,
but when
it fell the man stood bent,
sighed, shrugged,
and sighed again.

Birthright

My firstborn,
upon whom the fresh burst
of mother love was spent
in lavish joy:

Why has so much of what I held
dazzlingly before you
as bright and dear,
worthy of your trusting hand,
become for you so limp and dull,
like old discarded toys?

Instead, you grope impatiently
in the dark,
feeling for the jagged glass,
the rough, crude, ugly dangers
I had swept away,
to sense the torments
for yourself.

You walk the precipice,
scorning my hand,
daring the abyss
to make you giddy,
so far from me
I scarce could hear
a cry for help.

Once I kept a vigil
of the streets
and dragged your stubborn feet
to safety.
They are far too heavy now
for my slight frame,
and much too firmly fixed
upon this strange hard path
to manhood.

I still hold out
my treasures—
not gaudy baubles,
but all I value as worth handing on—
before your distant eyes.
I am weak and sick with fear
and cannot follow you,
nor am I welcome.

Inside you, somewhere,
gleam those gems
which you may one day claim
as your birthright.

▼

The Pride of Wholeness Blinds

The pride of wholeness blinds
me from an empathy
with frailty and flaw.
Perhaps the threat of blindness
crippling now my eyes
will open them to kindness.

Though Jesus healed the blind
by giving them clear eyes,
perhaps my vision's cure
requires some loss of sight—
a "losing of one's life"—
in order to find light.

▼

VII
Hope

▲

An Aged Easter

Lord,
Your fingers never felt the trembling
    of old age,
whose skills diminish day by solemn day
    until
the deftness once defining who we are
    before the world
is lost.

You have not felt the weakness closing in
    upon your frame,
when stairs become too steep,
    words too softly spoken,
light too dim,
    or the familiar road
stretched long.

You were not subject to the little vanities
    that puff our self-esteem,
so have been spared the mortifying loss
    of lavish chestnut hair,
a lithe physique, agility, or tutored strength,
    creativity, or learning earnestly
acquired.

Can compassion comprehend the terror
    of a fading memory—the losing
not simply of one's mind but one's whole self?
    To forget twelve dear disciples' names—
or was it ten? To wander lost in Nazareth;
    to feel abandoned and
abandoning?

Yet you
speak to and for us in this shadowed vale, uttering
    "My God, why hast thou forsaken me?"
on our behalf, and pray
    "Forgive them; for they know not
what they do." And you
    commit our death-bound spirits, Lord, into
God's hands.

A February Faith

In the winter of our life, after harvest,
flurried thoughts collect
in snowdrift memories,
covering sharp-edged truth
the way snow pillows soften rocks.

Like brittle trees
our old bones rasp;
we lean and sway in
the wild weather
of our winter winds.

Chilled, we shut out
the bustling world,
contract our dreams
to warm familiar hearths
where hopes can hibernate.
Through frosty panes
we glimpse a land grown alien,
muffled and remote.

Are we still locked in barren winter
even as the rivers thaw
and fecund soil gives birth,
when buds are bursting
and sweet breezes sing?
Or dare we face the final cold
with Easter courage,
like dormant seeds
that, through their burial,
enter into spring?

Spring: A Quibble on Words

"Spring" is too unsubtle
to describe
the rebirth of the earth.
The word suggests a bounding leap,
not the unobtrusive greening
of a tree
like a streetlight coming on.

Nor does it enunciate
the tender,
excruciating gentleness
of unfolding leaves,
whose unscarred primal beauty
stirs an anguished joy
and prompts a mad hope
that innocence
may yet prevail
in the world.

Bold azaleas, sturdy hyacinths,
warm roses, jolly jonquils
rise from the grim earth
to proclaim
the birth of beauty,
the fertility of hope,
life's unquenchable
joy.

Mother

I came to see you,
     but you were not there.
Your absence was so present
     that I gasped,
while looking at your unfamiliar,
     so familiar face.

(We close the eyes
     of people when they die,
because the emptiness
     unnerves and tells us
prematurely what we're not
     prepared to know.)

They say you left
     so quietly, as though
you just forgot to breathe
     the next sweet shallow breath.
So many of your memories had long
     been packed and sent ahead.

I gaze upon your stillness,
     feel you teaching, teaching me
the universal truth of love and loss.
     Child of your womb,
I'm drawn again into that shaping dark
     to mourn my new maturity.

False Expectations

Butterflies,
     caught in startling splendor
     in a see-through tomb,
so nearly live,
     poised upon a twig
     or hovering near a bud,
wear their cubes of plastic
     with eternal grace.

We search among the cubes in silence,
     not daring to admit
     even in the intimacy
        of mother and daughter
     our rash, unreasoned hope
        that somewhere
        in this mezzanine display
        for shoppers' lavish whims
     our butterfly awaits.

     "Our" butterfly,
        which I have never seen
        except through tremulous accounts
        you shared:
            of solace from its clinging wings
            upon your hand
            as you stepped heavily
            from Father's fresh-closed grave.
        How you laid it gently in the grass,
            and later met it winging
            through your door
               (months later,
               to be sure a different one,
               but still soft brown,
               marked like a signature in blue).
        Again it nuzzled unafraid
            within your palm
            and left you
              strangely comforted.

Our eyes scan anxiously
those plastic tombs,
and though I give mute contract
to our search,
I'm glad our lovely moth
    escaped the cubes.
We need no more reminders
    of the dead.
The message of our butterfly
    is life.

▼

Renascence

Oh, I have lost my first love.
    He's buried deep inside
the man whom now I cherish
    more than the youth who died.

Yes, he has lost his first love,
    for I have perished too.
Thus are we learning not to grieve
    for the dead who are born anew.